SNOW
MONKEYS

Wildlife Monographs – Snow Monkeys
Copyright © 2009 Evans Mitchell Books

Text and Photography Copyright
© 2009 Heather Angel

First published in the
United Kingdom in 2009 by:
Evans Mitchell Books
The Old Forge, Forge Mews
16 Church Street
Rickmansworth
Hertfordshire WD3 1DH
United Kingdom
www.embooks.co.uk

Design by:
Darren Westlake
TU ink Ltd, London
www.tuink.co.uk

British Library Cataloguing in Publication Data.
A CIP record of this book is available
on request from the British Library.

ISBN: 978-1-901268-37-9

Printed in China

SNOW MONKEYS

HEATHER ANGEL

Evans Mitchell Books

Contents

Introduction

Snow monkeys might appear to be something of a misnomer since monkeys are associated with living in warm climates rather than in sub-zero temperatures. But some Japanese macaques (*Macaca fuscata*) have adapted to living in a mountain region close to Nagano, where the 1998 Winter Olympics were held on the Island of Honshu. Here snow falls for one third of the year, hence the affectionate name of snow monkeys.

These monkeys live in a thermal valley known as Jigokudani (Hell's Valley), where steam vents emerge from the cliffs. Surprisingly, this apparently inhospitable location has become a winter paradise for the monkeys, because the natural hot water contained within a pool allows them to enjoy a hot soaking – even when it snows.

Japanese people have for long enjoyed bathing in a natural thermal bath known as an *onsen*. But only when the cover of the 30 January 1970 issue of *Life* magazine featured a snow-covered head emerging from the pool, did the western world become aware that monkeys also indulged in thermal bathing.

Right: Newborn snow monkey sits amongst fresh green herb layer at Jigokudani Monkey Park in June.

Opposite: A snow monkey grooms another in winter snow at Jigokudani.

The monkeys living at Jigokudani have been extensively studied and are now habituated to humans, who have to trek through the forest along snow-covered paths to reach the monkeys in winter. After the snow melts in spring, the monkeys move up into the trees to feast on blossom. A popular time for visitors to go to Jigokudani is early in June just after the females have given birth to their single offspring. During the first few days after the babies are born, they cling tightly to their mother, but gradually the distance of their forays increases as they explore their environment and learn to play with each other. Come the autumn, when the deciduous trees turn glorious shades of yellow and red, fruits, roots and mushrooms are the main food source.

Wildlife Monographs – Snow Monkeys reveals how these most northerly non-human primates live and survive in winter temperatures down to -15° C (5° F). The images here provide an intimate picture of the snow monkeys' way of life in the Japanese Alps through the seasons – whether foraging on leaves, flowers and seeds, leaping across a river, grooming or youngsters tumbling and sliding down snowy slopes. There are also rare images of a mother submerging into a hot pool with her frightened newborn clinging to her fur.

Above: A snow monkey relaxes whilst being groomed in the hot pool at Jigokudani.

Above: Japanese macaque calls out from rocky outcrop on Koshima Island.

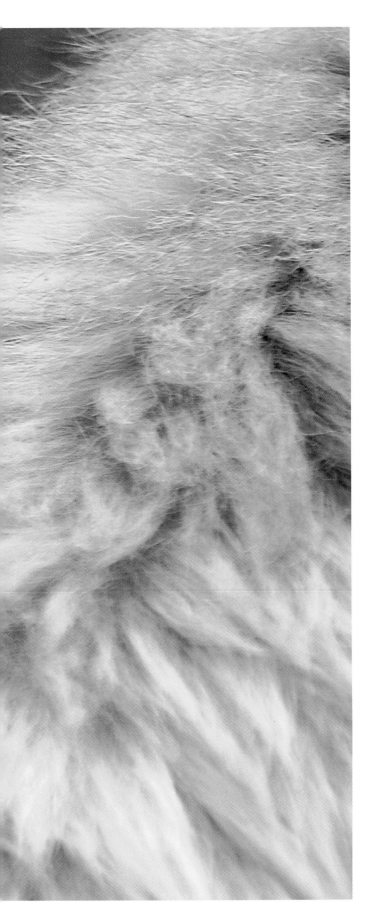

Read about the fascinating discoveries biologists have made from their field studies on Japan's only monkey, including how the primates can develop different accents and how monkeys in one troop have learnt to wash sweet potatoes in the sea before eating them.

Above: A group of snow monkeys huddle together in summer as a newborn yawns.

Left: Baby snow monkey with dark fur surfaces from hot pool beside dry mother.

History and distribution

The snow monkey or Japanese macaque – known as *Nihon zaru* in Japan – is one of 22 macaque species that occur within a wider range of climates and habitats than any other primate, apart from humans. All occur in Asia, except for the Barbary macaque (*Macaca sylvannus*) which lives in North Africa, plus a single colony on the Rock of Gibraltar.

It is thought that Japanese macaques originated from an Asian ancestor, either the same as or similar to that of the rhesus macaque (*Macaca mulatta*). Terrestrial animals were able to invade Japan via one or more land bridges which formed when the sea level dropped during glacial periods. One of these bridges which formed across the Korea Strait between the Korean Peninsula and Kyushu and west Honshu, is now submerged at a depth of 130 metres (426.5 feet).

Left: The rhesus macaque, which is thought to share a common ancestor with the Japanese macaque, has a longer tail – seen here as it checks out predators before drinking in a Chinese river.

Opposite: Snow monkeys relax in and beside the hot pool at Jigokudani in winter.

During periods of sea level lowering, the macaques could move on to shallow water islands offshore from Kyushu, Shikoku and Honshu. Today, monkeys still live on six small islands – Awajishima, Shodoshima, Kashima, Kinkazan, Koshima and Yakushima. However, they became extinct on three small islands – Omishima (north of west Honshu), Hiradoshima (north-west of Kyushu) and Tanegashima (north-east of Yakushima), where they died out as a result of deforestation in the twentieth century. The reasons why Japanese macaques have not invaded the northernmost island of Hokkaido are most probably because either there was no land bridge or the climate was too cold for them. Winter temperatures on Hokkaido plummet to – 25° C (-13° F), the season when Japanese cranes (*Grus japonensis*) perform their balletic courtship dances on the snow.

Two distinct sub-species of Japanese macaques are recognised today. *Macaca fuscata fuscata* is the mainland sub-species, which occurs throughout the three main islands and small islands with the exception of the southernmost location. Here, on Yakushima Island (60 kilometres or 37 miles, south of Kyushu), the endemic – and now protected – Yakushima macaques (*Macaca fuscata yakui*) are distinguished by their smaller size and darker fur.

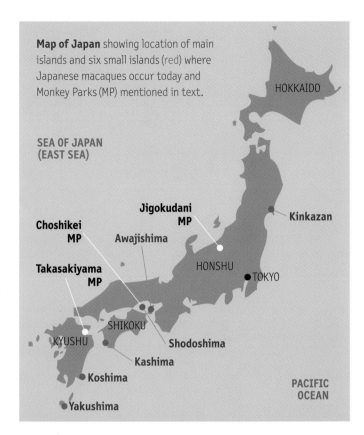

Map of Japan showing location of main islands and six small islands (red) where Japanese macaques occur today and Monkey Parks (MP) mentioned in text.

Right: A snow monkey walks down a monkey path over rocks in cleared forest habitat Jigokudani.

Above: Japanese macaques emerge from forest to feed on wheat provided by researchers on the sandy beach, Koshima Island.

Left: A pair of Japanese cranes performs their courtship dance in mid-winter on Hokkaido — Japan's northernmost island.

The macaques that live on the Shimokita Peninsula on the north-eastern tip of Honshu, represent the northernmost non-human primates in the world, but the most famous snow monkeys occur at an elevation of 800 metres (12,625 feet) in Jigokudani Monkey Park at Shiga Heights, also on Honshu. Here, the prolonged winter is alleviated by making daily dips in a thermal pool – the monkeys' own outside Jacuzzi!

As the size of Japanese macaque troops increases on the mainland, the monkeys spread out onto farmland where they feast on crops and are regarded as pests. The last survey, carried out in 1992 by the Environmental Agency of Japan (now Ministry of the Environment, Japan), recorded the presence or absence of monkeys in ten by ten kilometre square grids. It is estimated the current total population of Japanese macaques could be around 100,000 animals, but with several thousand pest monkeys being destroyed each year an up-to-date census is long overdue.

Snow monkeys and their behaviour have intrigued Japanese artists for centuries. Katsushika Hokusai (1760-1849), famous for his painting *The Great Wave*, painted the *Trained Monkey Eating Peaches* in 1848 – the Year of the Monkey – when he was almost ninety years old.

Monkeys were a favourite subject of the artist Mori Sosen (1747-1821) who worked during the Edo Period (1795-1801). There is a story that after he was criticised for the unrealistic way he depicted monkeys caught by hunters, which he painted in his garden, he ventured into the mountains to paint them in their natural habitat. He lived in the woods around Osaka for months, surviving on fruits and nuts, observing the intimate life of monkeys and produced some charming studies of them with flowers and fruits of the forest. We can see the macaques playing in a plum tree, beside a rose bush with a plucked rose and in a persimmon tree eating the fruit (page 39).

Opposite: Snow monkey mother and baby warm up in a hot pool during a snowstorm at Jigokudani. The baby remains reassuringly close to its mother.

Above: A painting by the Japanese artist Mori Sosen depicts Japanese macaques foraging for plum blossom in the spring.

Distinguishing features

The Japanese macaque is a semi-terrestrial Old World medium-sized monkey with fur that varies from brown to brown-grey or yellow-brown above and an underside that is much paler. Adults viewed face-on have their slightly pointed ears hidden by their long head hair, but the ears are visible on a side view of the head. They are most conspicuous when a macaque emerges from swimming underwater and the fine hairs become plastered to the body.

The forward-facing eyes provide binocular vision; this enables Japanese macaques to judge distances when moving quickly and to have good hand-eye co-ordination for capturing lively insect prey. They also have colour vision which helps them distinguish ripe fruit from unripe green fruit, which reduces foraging time.

However, their small nostrils and downward pointed noses result in a poor sense of smell. These monkeys have 20 milk teeth and 32 permanent teeth, which is the same as humans, but the 38.6° C (101° F) body temperature is slightly higher than humans.

Above: Profile of a snow monkey shows the flattened nose above the protruding jaws.

Opposite: A winter portrait of a snow monkey shows the red facial skin and forward facing eyes.

Top: Darker newborn snow monkey plays beside mother with much paler fur.

Above: Three baby snow monkeys huddle together in winter, each with distinct variations in their facial features.

Right: A dark-haired baby surfaces from hot pool showing plastered fine fur and large ears. Darker pigmented areas can be seen around the nipples and on the arms.

A striking feature of Japanese macaques is their pink to red, hairless faces; indeed, one of the French names is *macaque à face rouge*. Newborn snow monkeys have a uniform pale pink face, which gradually turns redder with age. Primatologists studying Japanese macaques can recognise individuals by their facial features, in the same way that individual humans can be distinguished. To the untrained eye, however, macaques are more difficult to separate because they don't have different coloured hair or hair styles. But each monkey has a different face: fights may leave distinctive scars or damaged noses and old females tend to develop a receding hairline.

Above: A scarred face.

Below: Old female with receding hairline, relaxes in her favourite spot in the hot pool.

One feature which varies amongst Japanese macaques is eye colour, which changes with age. Blue eyes occur most often in newborns, infants and the oldest monkeys. Juveniles and prime adults have pale brown to yellow eyes with pigments that are not present at birth and which degenerate with age. Research into the eye colour of Japanese macaques in their natural

Above: Yellow eyes of an adult snow monkey stare out from a red face.

habitat was done in Choshikei Monkey Park on Shodoshima and at Takasakiyama Monkey Park in Beppu on Kyushu. Photos of the eye colour were taken on sunny days when the pupils were contracted so that the iris filled most of the eye. Using a digital camera, a fixed white balance was used and the images taken when the monkeys looked directly towards the lens.

Adult faces become intensively red during the mating season, along with their bottoms and nipples. Sex hormones dilate blood capillaries under the skin which produces the deeper red colour. Also on the backsides are thickened cornified pads known as ischial callosities – quite simply sitting-pads – which help the monkeys to sit on surfaces for long periods. These pads are characteristic of Old World monkeys and some apes.

The main differences between the sexes are body size and weight and also the size of the canine teeth. Male monkeys are noticeably larger than females: the average weight of male Japanese macaques is 11.3 kilograms (24.9 pounds), whilst females have an average weight of 8.4 kilograms (18.5 pounds). Body weight tends to increase with latitude, so that monkeys living in northern, cooler regions are heavier than monkeys living in southern, warmer regions. Also, monkeys living in colder areas, such as Jigokudani, develop a thicker coat to withstand the sub-zero temperatures. In late spring and early summer the monkeys moult to produce a lightweight summer coat.

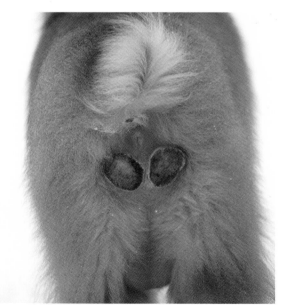

Above: Female Japanese macaque cradles her baby on Koshima.

Left: The rear view of an adult snow monkey with raised tail shows the red bottom with the calloused rump that allows the monkeys to sit for long periods.

Opposite: An alpha male or 'boss' monkey rests on a rocky outcrop above the beach on Koshima in April.

Top: Long-tailed macaque walks on beach in Ujung Kulon National Park, Indonesia, showing long tail.

Above: The short tail can be seen on a baby snow monkey.

Above right: The male northern pigtail macaque (*Macaca nemestrina*) has a particularly striking face.

Unlike bonnet macaques (*Macaca radiata*) from southern India or long-tailed macaques (*Macaca fascicularis*) from south-east Asia, Japanese macaques are stump-tailed monkeys. Their short tails which are a further adaptation to the cold climate, average just over nine centimetres (approximately 3.5 inches) in males and slightly less in females. Newborn monkeys have a short and thin rat-like tail. Short, stubby tails are of no help to macaques when they climb trees.

Clockwise from top left: A Japanese macaque looks down as it crosses the Yokoyu River using a tree trunk bridge in Jigokudani.

A snow monkey leaps across the Yokoyu River at Jigokudani.

Snow monkeys can swim well.

Footprints of a snow monkey after a light snowfall.

A snow monkey lives up to its name as it runs through deep snow in winter.

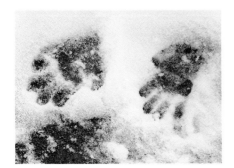

When not sitting to forage or groom, Japanese macaques move around on all four limbs, walking or running. They can run at speed to escape from danger and also leap across streams or wet areas of sand. If need be, these macaques are efficient swimmers. In 1970 a young male monkey was seen to swim over 950 kilometres (367 miles) from Koshima Island to Torishima, another island further out to sea.

Japanese macaques climb trees to feed on foliage or bark in winter, flowers in summer and fruits in autumn. They may also climb trees to sleep on a branch against the trunk of a Japanese cedar during a snow storm, when they cluster together to keep warm. The technique for climbing a large trunk is to hug the tree and to alternate the arms for the climb. Powerful hind feet with widely spaced out toes help them to grasp trunks and branches. The descent is made bottom first. Females tend to spend more time up trees than the males.

When a mother with a newborn baby wants to make a speedy getaway, she clutches the infant to her belly before taking off in a lop-sided three-limbed run. If an object – such as a fruit or a snow ball – is held in both hands, Japanese macaques are able to stand up and walk on their hind legs. Their hands are like those of humans, with opposable thumbs for gripping objects more efficiently. They are used not only to deftly pick up small objects, but also for plucking eggs of fur lice when grooming. The eggs are simply disposed by eating them. Snow monkeys sometimes stand up when calling to get a clearer view of a confrontation.

Right: A baby snow monkey stands up to eat frozen snow like an ice lolly held in both hands.

Above: An alert Japanese macaque stands up on a rock outcrop on Koshima to gain a better view of an incident.

Right sequence: A snow monkey climbs a Japanese cedar (*Cryptomeria japonica*) by hugging the trunk to reach a convenient branch where it can forage on bark in winter.

Habitat and diet

Japanese macaques spend most of their time living within forests from sea level up to an elevation of 1,500 metres (4,920 feet), spanning latitudes between 30°15' N and 41°30' N. The type of forest varies with latitude and elevation, from deciduous broadleaf and evergreen to subtropical and subalpine. However, apart from the island of Koshima off the southernmost island of Kyushu, most of the monkeys live in mountain forests, because the lower levels of their range have been cleared and developed.

These monkeys are diurnal (active during the day) and they spend almost a quarter of each day feeding in separate bouts – usually two or three times per day. Their natural food varies with the habitat, the season and temperature. During the winter, the diet of monkeys living at higher altitudes – where deciduous trees shed their leaves and snow carpets the ground for up to one third of the year – is much more limited. For example at Jigokudani, where snow can lie for 140 days building up to a depth of 250 centimetres (8.2 feet) snow monkeys have a harsh time finding food. Early on, when the snow is not too deep, they can grub up roots from the ground.

Opposite: The forest habitat of snow monkeys at Jigokudani in June.

Right: Snow monkey walks through heavy snow in Jigokudani.

After a succession of heavy snowfalls, the monkeys climb trees for winter buds; but their major natural winter food source is bark, which is stripped from various wild trees including elm, ash, maple, spindle, dogwood, cherry, oak, pine, larch as well as a Japanese cedar plantation. Sometimes if the bark does not readily peel, adults will eat branches, while infants eat more manageable twigs. In other parts of Japan where there is less snow in winter, much less bark is eaten and in the evergreen subtropical forest on Koshima, bark eating is practically non-existent.

Right: The tips of Japanese cedar branches are eaten by snow monkeys in winter; such fibre-rich foods are digested via fermentation in an enlarged caecum and colon.

Below: Humans are not the only primates which suffer from pollen allergies, some Japanese macaques are allergic to the pollen released by the male cones of Japanese cedar.

Opposite: A juvenile snow monkey eats Japanese cedar bark in Jigokudani.

Throughout the year at Jigokudani, the monkeys are fed with grain and apples, but when there is plenty of natural food, from spring to autumn, the monkeys spend much less time at the feeding ground on the river-beach than during the winter. At this time of year, the grain thrown onto the snow and into the hot pool must make a welcome change to their monotonous natural diet of bark. The monkeys spend some time collecting the barley, one grain at a time. Apples are also provided but the monkeys have to work harder to reach them – either in a bucket on a long string hung from a wire or in the centre of a long Perspex tube. The only way they can retrieve the apple from the tube is by finding a stick long enough to poke it out.

Above: A snow monkey dives into the hot pool to retrieve soya beans.

Above: Using both hands to feed on grain gathered from the snow.

Left: A Jigokudani snow monkey has learnt to use a tool – a long stick – to retrieve an apple from inside a Perspex tube.

Opposite: When grain is scattered on snow at Jigokudani in winter, the snow monkeys may have some initial squabbles, but soon space out to peacefully feed.

Top left: Japanese butterbur, an early spring perennial, is eaten not only as a vegetable but also by Japanese macaques.

Top right: Wild cherry blossom or Yamazakura is one of several kinds of tree blossom that Japanese macaques feed on in the spring, here with young bronze leaves.

Above: A rocky overhang makes a convenient place for snow monkeys to shelter beneath whilst feeding when rain or snow falls.

Between January and April the macaques move around and forage amongst the sunny deciduous forests on the south slope of Hell's Valley. As the temperature rises after April, the monkeys begin to move across to the cooler north slope to forage. Bark-eating ceases after the April thaw, as herbaceous plants begin to sprout on the forest floor. Then the snow monkeys seek out buds and blossoms of wildflowers, including those of Japanese butterbur (*Petasites japonicus*). As buds begin to burst on the deciduous trees, forays are once again made up trees – to feed on buds and new leaves of elm, beech and maple. Snow monkeys will even feast on tree blossom, such as wild cherry, before it fully opens and while it still contains nectar. Older monkeys return to their favourite trees from past seasons, remembering a convenient fork on which they can sit and stretch out for leaves or flowers.

Throughout the summer, Japanese macaques feed on plants as well as any birds' eggs or insects they find. Come the autumn, they feast on protein-rich foods such as seeds, fruits and berries, fungi and even insects on Kinkazan Island (in north-west Honshu). These foods help to build up body reserves during the leanest season, especially in snow-covered locations.

Top: Japanese dogwood (*Cornus kousa*) fruits are one of many kinds eaten by Japanese macaques and their colour vision enables them to speedily select the ripe fruits which are sniffed and licked before they are eaten.

Left: As baby snow monkeys begin to explore, they touch and smell wild plants, sometimes putting them in their mouth. Gradually, they learn what is safe to eat by watching their mother.

37

Above: Wild *Camellia japonica* flowers are eaten by Japanese macaques on Koshima Island.

Above right: Inside the forest on Koshima Island, the best place to see macaques is on the monkey paths.

Like all macaques, snow monkeys have cheek pouches used to rapidly collect and temporarily store food, where it can be chewed at a more leisurely pace; if necessary away from competitors, predators or in a more comfortable place out of the wind, rain or snow. After leaving fruiting trees, monkeys eat the edible parts of the fruits, spitting out the seeds from the cheek pouch. Studies on macaques in the warm temperate evergreen forest on Yakushima Island have shown that the habit of carrying fruits in cheek pouches helps to disperse seeds from fruiting trees. Fruits with smaller seeds get dispersed via droppings; whereas fruits with seeds over 10 millimetres (0.4 inches) are seldom swallowed by the monkeys, instead they are spat out and dispersed, typically in sunny places which the monkeys favour.

In southern locations, Japanese macaques feed on herbaceous plants in winter and also on nuts, which are left in preference to seeds and fruits in autumn. Seasonal variation in the feeding behaviour of eight adult Japanese macaques was studied over an 18-month period on the island of Yakushima. During a complete calendar year in the evergreen forest just over a third of the foraging time was spent gathering leaves and roots, with almost as much time finding fleshy fruit. Additionally, seeds, flowers, invertebrates and fungi made up the rest of the diet. Monkeys collecting fruits up in the trees inevitably drop some, providing an easy meal for deer following beneath. When feeding on leaves, the monkeys spent less time moving around, whereas finding fruits or insects involved more foraging time. After macaques have eaten and drunk they seek a sunny place in cool weather or a shady spot in hot weather to rest.

Another study on Yakushima has shown how habitat influences the diet of Japanese macaques. Within a high-altitude mixed forest, with just over half the area covered by conifers, almost half of the annual feeding time was spent eating fibre-rich mature leaves, with fruit, seeds, flowers and fungi making up the balance. Whereas in the warmer coastal forest on the same island, the emphasis was on fruits and seeds, with much less time spent on fibre-rich food, flowers and fungi. When the temperature was low, the macaques ate more fibre-rich foods such as mature leaves and fern fronds, rather than leaves from trees which require using up precious energy climbing trees. Also herbs tend to flourish in sunny places (such as logged areas) where the macaques can soak up warming rays whilst eating.

Above: A painting by the Japanese artist Mori Sosen shows Japanese macaques foraging for persimmon fruit (*Diospyros kaki*) in the autumn. The cheek pouches are clearly visible on the macaque holding the fruit.

Above: A monkey eats a sweet potato washed in the sea with another soil-covered potato on the rock.

Opposite: A Japanese macaque carries a sweet potato to the sea for washing on Koshima Island and another eats a potato after washing it.

Unusual foods eaten by some Japanese macaques include *takenigusa*, a bamboo-like grass that contains toxic alkaloids used in Chinese medicine to treat parasitic infections. In Arashiyama, to counteract the high-energy low-fibre foods which tend to lead to stomach upsets, the macaques also eat soil – a habit known as geophagy – containing clay minerals that prevent diarrhoea. Yet at Katsuyama (south-west Honshu) macaques have been observed to carry and wash soil from the roots of grasses; others rubbed dirt from the roots by rolling the grasses along a flat rock beside a river. This grass washing is the first account of the monkeys washing natural food; although one troop of Japanese macaques have long been known to wash food provided by primatologists to lure them out of their forest habitat on Koshima Island.

On a hot day in September 1953, unwashed sweet potatoes were left on the shady beach on Koshima at some distance from water. Satsue Mito, a primary school teacher who was a local assistant to the primatologists, saw an 18-month old female monkey – later christened Imo (Japanese for sweet potato) – collect a potato and carry it to a stream where she washed it before eating. Gradually Imo's mother and juvenile macaques learnt to wash potatoes. After four and a half years, 18 percent of adult monkeys over eight years old and 79 percent of the juveniles had learnt to wash potatoes by imitating Imo. By 1961, all monkeys in the troop, apart from one born after 1950, washed potatoes. Later on, the monkeys took the potatoes to the sea to wash them – presumably they liked their potatoes seasoned with salt!

Right: A troop of Japanese macaques feed on wheat provided by researchers on a sandy beach, Koshima Island; some monkeys are washing sand from the grain in the stream.

Opposite: In warmer months, Japanese macaques feed in the Yokoyu River at Jigokudani, turning over stones in search of frogs and aquatic insects.

In 1956, Imo found she could separate wheat grains from sand when the grain was scattered on the beach. After she scooped them up and dropped them into water, the sand grains sank while the wheat grains floated. Other monkeys in Imo's troop also learnt this behaviour. Gulls, renowned as scavengers the world over, were not slow to catch on to the provisioned food and hung around in the hope of picking up any leftovers.

But food washing is by no means unique to the Koshima troop. It developed quite separately at Jigokudani; after they were given apples, some monkeys began to wash them either in a pool (see page 51) or in the river or in snow during the winter.

Providing food on Koshima led to a rapid increase in the macaque population, but when provisioning was reduced, some males began eating dead fish. Over a period of six years, this addition to their diet spread throughout most of the group. Elsewhere, macaques living near the coast have been seen to come down to the seashore to feed on crabs and shellfish.

Japanese macaques regularly eat live insects and spiders as well as snails, but predation of live vertebrates was thought to be a very rare occurrence. But there have now been several sightings of live frogs, skinks and lizards being preyed upon by Yakushima monkeys. The prey, which was attacked by an adult, was not always devoured completely but on several occasions the monkeys were seen to eat leaves after eating the flesh – a habit which has also been observed in chimpanzees.

So whether foraging in the wild or feeding on food provided by researchers, Japanese macaques are adaptable and opportunistic and will readily take advantage of an unexpected bounty that turns up by chance.

Behaviour and lifestyle

Like all monkeys that live within forests, studying the behaviour of Japanese macaques, their hierarchy and how they interact within a troop as a whole, initially proved difficult. The monkeys were glimpsed only for short periods in open glades or along monkey paths before they disappeared deep into the forest. Primatologists began studying a troop of macaques living in Arashiyama forest on Mount Watayama near Kyoto in 1954; after part of the forest was felled, they began to put out sweet potatoes in January 1955. It took a few weeks for the monkeys to find the food, but by February and March, when natural food is scarce to come by, the potatoes began to disappear. Several more provisioning sites – as scientists call the feeding areas – were set up so the monkeys could be observed out in the open.

The macaques thrived so well on the extra food that the initial troop of some 50 animals in 1954 had grown to 163 by March 1966. By June the troop split in two; one staying on the mountain, while the other spread out and began to invade settled areas, including shrines.

Left: Newborn snow monkey looks for reassurance towards mother busy feeding.

Opposite: A newborn snow monkey grasps mother's legs and gains shelter from sun beneath her body.

Above: An alpha male rests on rock with youngster behind.

Opposite: Three snow monkeys groom one another in thermal pool.

Detailed studies at Arashiyama, at Shiga Heights, on Koshima Island and other locations produced family trees from which the hierarchy could be determined. It was discovered that Japanese macaques have a matrilineal society, with the alpha female being succeeded by the youngest, not the oldest, daughter. Within this society, several generations of females – grandmothers, aunts, cousins, sisters, and nieces – all help with caring and grooming of young babies once they no longer cling to their mother day and night. There is also an alpha male or 'boss' monkey within each troop. Most often a

male macaque acquires alpha status as a result of the death or departure of the previous alpha male; but if the 'boss' monkey loses his rank or the troop splits up, both these scenarios open up a new alpha male position.

In between feeding, bathing or moving Japanese macaques spend much time grooming. This practical activity keeps the fur in good condition by separating matted fur, thereby allowing ventilation to the skin – essential in hot weather since Japanese macaques are unable to pant or sweat. Another benefit of grooming is that it functions as an appeasement gesture by helping to relieve stress as a result of competition for food or territory. Grooming also reinforces bonding between a mother and her infant, between siblings and other members of the group. The size of the troop does not seem to affect how many different individuals are groomed by one animal. Research on a troop containing 84 females, found that each female groomed on average ten others yet half of them spend 50 percent of their time with just one grooming partner. The higher the rank of the snow monkey, the longer the time spent grooming it.

Macaques also benefit from grooming by having louse eggs removed from their fur. These parasites occur most often on the back, outer arms and legs, which may determine which parts of the body macaques groom most frequently. It was estimated that a single female macaque can carry 550 louse eggs, so regular grooming is essential to keep the lice in check.

During the winter months, snow monkeys tend to move around much less, preferring instead to soak up heat by sunning themselves by day. Because a troop is constantly on the move, they seek out a different place to sleep at the end of each day. Often this is up on a solid branch where it joins a tree trunk. In winter, they prefer deciduous trees, because snow-laden conifer branches – such as Japanese cedar – can shed snow on the monkeys causing a reduction in their body heat. The macaques also huddle together on the ground seeking some shelter behind a fallen tree or rocks; as the temperature plummets, so the huddle size increases.

Left: Snow monkey uses teeth to remove tenacious dirt or lice from hair.

Above: A mother with her newborn plus older juveniles huddle together as they sleep.

It is no coincidence that places where free handouts have been given to the macaques, are where food washing and hot pool bathing have been developed. This readily accessible food cuts down time spent foraging, thereby providing time for the monkeys to develop cultural activities.

The development of potato and wheat washing has already been covered on pages 41-42. When scientists at Jigokudani offered apples to the monkeys, they too began to wash them and one monkey chose to wash his apples by rolling them in the snow. Some scientists believe such novel behaviour is observed and passed on by an offspring copying a parent, from an infant to a parent or from one adult to another, so that a tradition or 'culture' gradually permeates through the group. Other people argue the behaviour is discovered quite independently.

The thermal valley at Shiga Heights provided a source of natural hot water for an open air *onsen* or hot tub, popular with Japanese visitors. In the 1950s, after the temperature was lowered, one female snow monkey hopped into the hot tub. After this, it was decided to build an *onsen* especially for the snow monkeys.

Above: Hot pool heaven: snow monkeys relax in hot pool.

Right: A snow monkey washes an apple in hot pool before eating it.

Above: As the steam rises, a snow monkey enjoys an outdoor sauna at Jigokudani.

Right: A mother with her bedraggled newborn baby in the hot pool.

Like humans, the way the snow monkeys enter the pool relates to their age. Youngsters rush up to the edge, invariably doing a honey pot dive, splashing all around them as they hit the water before completely submerging; whereas older female monkeys climb in slowly backwards until their feet rest on the bottom, so their head hair is kept dry. They then either wade out to join other monkeys, where they may mutually groom, or to their favourite spot, ending up draping their arms over the edge of the pool. One old female would spend day after day during the winter in the same position until she died. After submergence, monkeys come up with their hair plastered to their bodies, but a quick flick of the head removes most of the water and the hair soon fluffs out again. When monkeys climb out of the pool with flattened hair their comparatively slender body size then becomes apparent.

Taking an outdoor Jacuzzi is a seasonal pastime for the snow monkeys and by checking out the webcam throughout the year it can be seen that only a few monkeys enter the pool during the summer, invariably to retrieve soya beans either by bending down with their hands or diving down to the bottom. They also visit the pool year round to drink after they have fed; most often they walk along the rim and bend down to drink with their haunches up in the air. Energetic monkeys will leap onto one of the emergent stepping stones in the centre of the pool to drink. A mother clutches her newborn as she bends down to drink, often submerging it. At Jigokudani they also drink at the edge of the river when it is not in flood. When the macaques are on the sandy beach at Koshima they drink from a freshwater stream.

Top: A snow monkey shakes off water by twisting the head.

Above: On surfacing, a snow monkey wipes fur from its face.

Left: Snow monkey walks on snow after emerging from hot pool.

Above: Snow monkey reflected in hot pool as it bends down to drink, after bathing up to its neck.

Left: As a mother drinks in the hot pool her newborn baby gets dunked, as it remains firmly grasping her fur.

Above: A young snow monkey uses a stone as a play object.

Below: Three baby snow monkeys size up a snowball.

Below right: A baby bites bark from a twig.

Another example of a behaviour that has developed within Japanese macaques in more than one location is stone playing. Initially spotted by a primatologist at Arashiyama in 1979, when a female was playing with stones. Just four years later, half of the group were playing by banging stones together and on roofs, clearly fascinated by the noise this made. Unlike the material advantage of food washing or bathing in a hot pool in cold weather, stone-playing appears to be an activity that macaques do simply to pass away the time.

Infant snow monkeys, like any primate, also enjoy playing with objects. From midsummer when they are born until snow begins to fall, their most common play objects are sticks and stones. Sticks are picked up and chewed or thrown, while stones are turned over, thrown and even tasted.

But after snow blankets the ground, any loose stones or sticks become buried. So then the infant snow monkeys begin to play with lumps of ice or snow. Some are picked up and licked (see page 28) while others accumulate more snow as they are kicked around. In this way snowballs are created which youngsters carry around and fight over.

Above: Baby snow monkey carries snowball at Jigokudani.

On clear winter days youngsters enjoy playing on sunny slopes where saplings emerge from the snow. Here they swing on the branches, their falls cushioned by the snow in which they tumble over one another. They also take advantage of well worn pathways cut through the snow, using them as natural slides.

As an infant macaque develops, sight becomes one of the major senses with the eyes providing sharp vision and a sense of perspective as well as the ability to see colour. Hearing is also good, although unlike an antelope, the ears cannot twist around to pick up the source of the sound; instead young macaques have to learn to twist their head towards the sound source. The high level of visual acuity has been developed at the expense of their sense of smell, with Japanese macaques having a small nose with close-set down-turned nostrils.

Above: Baby snow monkeys playfight in the snow.

Opposite: Wet baby snow monkey after emerging from hot pool with fine hairs plastered onto body – turning head to pick up sounds from left of shot.

Monkeys communicate within their group both visually and vocally. Researchers who spend long periods making field observations and who know the hierarchy within a group are much more alive to the varied signals, but some are easy to spot. When a monkey brings the corners of the mouth forward to form a circular open mouth, covering the teeth, this is threatening behaviour. Other threatening visual signals include ear-flattening, brow-raising to reveal the

white skin and ear-erecting. When the teeth are bared to form a grimace, this shows subordinate behaviour. Yet when the teeth are visible but closed together this fear grimace is used as a means of reducing aggression.

Above: A call with an open mouth displaying the teeth conveys subordinate behaviour.

Opposite: A call with an open circular mouth that hides the teeth is a threat call.

61

Humans are known to acquire distinct dialects in different parts of a single country and researchers have discovered that Japanese macaques also have distinct vocal variations in different habitats. Female monkeys maintain vocal contact with each other by making repeated cooing calls; these were recorded from 1990-1998 in two groups originally part of the same Yakushima troop until they were separated in 1956. While one group remained in evergreen forest on Yakushima Island, the other group was relocated 700 kilometres (434 miles) north to Mount Ohira on Honshu. The calls made by monkeys on Yakushima were found to be pitched much higher, so they could be heard through the tall forest trees which tend to block lower pitched calls; whereas lower pitched calls travelled easily across an open range with stunted vegetation on Mount Ohira.

Above: A snow monkey calls as it runs through the snow.

Opposite: Female snow monkey stands up and calls at Jigokudani.

Reproduction and growing up

Female Japanese macaques remain with their birth group forming a matrilineal society; whereas most of the males leave before they become sexually mature. They may live a solitary life before joining a new group or troop; they even move from one group to another. A single troop comprises about one third each of females and juveniles, with the remaining males and infants together making up the final third. Troop size is, however, very variable and can be as little as eight or as much as 166. Female Japanese macaques do not come into heat (oestrus) until they are 3.5 years old on average and males become sexually mature about a year later. Both male and female macaques are promiscuous, each having several partners during a single breeding season which lasts for several months from September to April. However, a female macaque will avoid mating with a previous mate for a second time. This means that the longer a male remains within a troop, his choice of mates is reduced. But this strategy ensures that genetic diversity is increased, at the same time reducing the odds of inbreeding.

Above right: Mother snow monkey suckles her baby.

Opposite: Baby snow monkey rides on mother's back in Jigokudani.

During the mating season, distinct skin colour changes can be seen on both males and females. When a female macaque (especially an older one) is on heat her red face becomes more intense in colour (sometimes referred to as 'sex skin'); as does the skin around her bottom. Both the faces and genitalia of the males also turn deep red and their tail is held erect so the genitals are more clearly visible.

It is the female which determines the choice of mate so that when two males compete for a female, the winner is not assured of a successful mating, unless he is most attractive to the female. After finding a male she prefers, she stays close to him, for a day or more, avoiding other males. He may groom her before mounting in response to the female presenting herself by standing up and looking back over the shoulder at her potential mate. Alternatively, she may walk backwards towards the male. He usually mounts her from behind using his two front limbs to clasp the back of the female while his feet grasp her legs. Japanese macaques can mate on the ground or in trees and a female may clutch her baby to her chest as a male mounts her. The male is silent during mating, whereas the female makes distinctly different sounds prior to mating (cooing) and during copulation (cackling).

Top: Male snow monkey grooms female prior to mating.

Above: Snow monkeys mate on a winter's day in Jigokudani.

Left: The red skin on the bottom of both male and female monkeys appears more vivid during the mating season.

Above: The red-skinned face of a female snow monkey becomes even more intense when she is on heat.

Gestation is normally five to six months (165 days); the birth times varying with the location and the group, but most babies are born from March to June with some as late as September. The behaviour of the mother changes on the day of the birth, which takes place on the ground. She spends less time grooming and moving around to forage for food, but more time resting. She seeks out a private place away from the main group activity, rejects other monkeys coming to groom her and avoids contact with other males. Before the birth, leaves and shoots form the main food source, whereas after the birth fruits are selected. These are easier to digest and they also provide more energy for the nursing mother. The average birth weight of the single baby is 540 grams (1.2 pounds), with male babies averaging slightly less than females. Immediately after birth, she licks her infant to initiate the mother-infant bond and also eats the placenta. Babies are born with a dark natal coat, which gradually lightens with age and have wide open eyes, but it takes a few days before they can follow moving objects.

The mother-infant bond is so strong that if a baby dies the mother carries the corpse with her for several days. On Koshima, one mother held onto her dead baby for a staggering 59 days during which time it became mummified. This behaviour, however, depends on the age of the dead infant. If it is older than three months the mother does not carry it. Also, miscarried babies and stillborn infants tend to be abandoned, although during filming of Japanese macaques, a mother was seen to give birth to a stillborn baby which she carried around for three days and nights, taking it up into a tree at night and screaming. Mothers which lose their babies have been known to attempt to steal another baby.

Top: A baby sits on the head of its mother.

Above: A newborn stretches up to touch its mother's face.

Opposite: Newborn snow monkey peeks out from mother's arm.

From observations on captive macaques, it has been found that female Japanese macaques do not raise their infants instinctively but have to learn this skill. When a female macaque was separated from her mother at birth and raised on her own, she did not know how to nurse her own newborn, with the result that her baby died.

A newborn macaque has remarkably large hands and feet for its size, for as soon as it is born it has to cling tightly to its mother – whether she is sitting or moving around on all fours. At first, it clings to her belly where it has ready access to her teats and can suckle whenever it needs food. In this position, it also gets carried ventrally with the mother clasping it to her belly before she gets up to move off in a three-legged run.

Above: Newborn snow monkey uses outsized foot – longer than face – to scratch.

Right: Snow monkey mother carries her newborn clinging to her belly.

Opposite: Newborn snow monkey sits beside mother showing large hand.

For the first month, most of the time is spent feeding and sleeping – even falling asleep with the nipple still in its mouth. As the infant develops, it climbs down from the mother so it can begin to crawl, but should an adult macaque approach which is not closely related the mother will snatch it back. By 20 days the babies begin to toddle and as they become sturdier on their feet they can interact and play with other babies, climbing onto rocks and shrubs. When babies are a month old, they begin to climb onto their mother's back, as this is more comfortable than having their body accidentally knocked against the ground when clinging on below. Initially, the baby clings precariously onto the back with all four limbs, but as muscles develop it learns to ride jockey-like which provides an elevated viewpoint of the surroundings. Baby macaques begin to eat solid food when they are five to six weeks old and by seven weeks are able to forage on their own.

Above sequence: Newborn is reluctant to let go of its grip on mother's fur as it descends headfirst to the ground.

Below sequence: Newborn scrambles up onto mother's back.

Opposite: Newborn attempts to escape from mother's clutch.

After three to four months babies go through a rebellious stage as they are torn between wanting to become independent and yet still being dependent on their mother. If they fail a task they may begin to cry and give up trying. This is when a mother will discipline her baby by pushing it to the ground or even giving it a harmless bite rather than give in to a tantrum.

Another duty of not only the mother but any nearby macaque, is to defend a baby from attack by a predator. This may be from above by an aerial predator such as a mountain hawk eagle (*Spizaetus nipalensis*), or from the ground by feral dogs and raccoon dogs (*Nyctereutes procyonoides*).

Female infants tend to be more sociable and groom more often than males, who prefer to play more energetically in larger groups. At seven months old, the mother begins to discourage the infant macaque from suckling. This is reinforced more emphatically by the time the infant is one year old. She does this either by covering her nipples or moving away. Females which have produced several offspring can be identified by their elongated nipples, stretched repeatedly by infants turning their head away from their mother whilst still retaining the nipple in their mouth.

Left: Snow monkey mother with her baby riding on her back walks through deep snow in Jigokudani.

Above: A newborn snow monkey tastes a wild plant at Jigokudani.

Opposite: Baby snow monkey stretches a mother's nipple when it turns its head.

From observations of a mother on Yakushima Island, maternal behaviour is quite different when her baby is unable to drink her milk. As the baby followed her mother through the forest, it screamed for help, but she ignored it and not long afterwards the baby died. Nursing a baby draws on a mother's body reserves and maybe she sensed it was not worth the effort for a baby which had no chance of surviving?

Above: Baby snow monkeys frolic in the snow and contest a snowball.

Above: Newborn snow monkeys learn by playing together.

During a visit to Jigokudani in early June, I observed how a mother's instinct to feed appeared to be stronger than her maternal instinct. Snow monkeys dive into the hot pool to retrieve soya beans thrown in by researchers. More than once, I saw a mother with a small baby clinging to her belly, not even hesitate as she dived into the water to feed. I could see the baby crawl up onto the back of its mother torn between its natural instincts to cling on tightly and surface to breathe. By releasing the grip of both hands and one foot it was still able to hang on yet stretch up towards the surface to gasp some air. When the mother had finished feeding and surfaced, she turned round, grasped her baby and placed it on her belly before climbing out. She then allowed it to suckle before moving away from the pool.

Left: A newborn snow monkey is torn between hanging on to mother's fur and letting go to rise up to breathe at the surface of the hot pool.

Below: Newborn snow monkey surfaces to breathe after mother dived into hot pool.

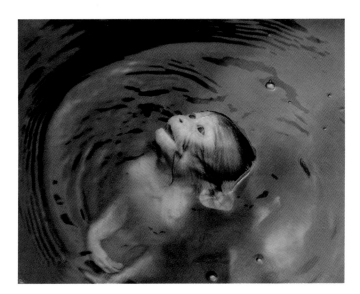

Above: On a sandy beach at low tide on Koshima Island a juvenile Japanese macaque peers around its mother.

A female gives birth to one offspring every two or three years and during her lifetime can produce up to nine babies. The peak time for producing offspring is when she is from 10-19 years old. Menopause occurs in older females as the number of menstrual cycles decrease each year during the third decade of her life.

Above: Young snow monkeys rest awhile after an active spell rushing around.

Snow monkeys and people

At the time Japanese macaques reached Japan via land bridges (from fossil evidence sometime between the middle to late Pleistocene Epoch), forests covered the islands and it must have been monkey heaven – that was until mankind arrived. Human activities threaten endemic monkey populations in many ways; most obviously by hunting and loss of habitat.

Another way in which the natural gene pool of macaques is threatened is by interbreeding with other macaque species. Some Taiwanese macaques (*Macaca cyclopsis*) which escaped from an animal collection in 1955 in Wakayama Prefecture on Honshu, mated with Japanese macaques to produce a hybrid population. The tail length of the hybrid animals is intermediate between that of the Japanese and Taiwanese macaques. Female Japanese macaques have also been known to mate with male rhesus macaques.

Left: Young rhesus macaque in Yunnan, China, has given its name to the rhesus antigens found in their blood.

Opposite: Sub-tropical forest covers most of Koshima, one of several islands inhabited by Japanese macaques.

Snow monkeys, as well as sika deer (*Cervus nippon*), wild boar (*Sus scrofa leucomystax*) and the Japanese serow (*Capricornis crispus*), all suffered from hunting until the Japanese Government placed a hunting ban on various wild mammals in 1948. This was the year the study of Japanese macaques began on Koshima Island after Kinji Imanishi (1902-1992) spotted a troop of wild monkeys whilst working on wild horses on Kyushu. The year 2008 was therefore the sixtieth anniversary of the founding of primate study in Japan.

Imanishi had been working on wild horses in Mongolia during the Second World War and he applied the same method he used there to the macaques. Individual monkeys were identified and named by Imanishi and his co-workers in 19 sites over a period of seven years, until the monkeys became habituated to their presence. The method of long term observations has become the standard way that non-human primates are studied in the field.

The Primate Research Group was set up in 1951 at Kyoto University, in the same year as the Koshima group of monkeys were first given sweet potatoes. Indeed, it was Japanese primatologists who first discovered and recorded the existence of matrilineal hierarchy in an Old World monkey – the Japanese macaque – long before the famous 1960's and 1970's studies undertaken by Jane Goodall and Dian Fossey on apes in Africa.

Above: As a Japanese tourist prepares to land on Koshima Island with shoes in his hand, a Japanese macaque sits on the bow of the boat.

Right: Japanese macaque eats a sweet potato after washing it in the sea, Koshima Island.

Opposite: Troop of Japanese macaques feed on wheat along edge of stream provided by researchers on sandy beach, Koshima Island.

Above: A newborn looks quizzically at its unresponsive mother at rest.

Right: Baby snow monkeys appear especially cute a few weeks after they are born, while they still have their delicate, dark natal fur and when they begin to make short forays away from their mother.

After the Japan Monkey Centre was opened in 1956 it began to publish the journal *Primates* (initially in Japanese but later in English) and the pioneering work of Japanese scientists became known to the western world. The opening of the Kyoto University Primate Research Institute, a decade later, greatly expanded research on Japanese macaques, as well as great apes in Africa and New World monkeys. This centre is now one of the largest primate centres in the world.

The practice of providing food to lure macaques out of the forest for study, gave rise to population increases, which happened to coincide with forests being cleared for development or replanting with coniferous monocultures, thereby causing fragmentation of the monkeys' natural forest habitat. More monkeys and less natural food made them venture outside forests in search of alternative food. Crops on farmland were an easy target, with citrus fruit being popular on Yakushima. The macaques are therefore regarded as a pest by farmers and a nuisance in suburbs. Farmers have tried several ways of deterring monkeys from gaining access to crops. Electric fencing is one solution, but is expensive. Another solution is to erect fencing with gaps where infra-red triggers are set; any monkey that enters, breaks the beam and sets off an explosive device. But some monkeys now ignore the noise.

Even though Japanese macaques are supposed to be protected, if anyone claims for personal or property damage caused by a wild monkey, a permit is issued locally for its capture or culling. Inevitably farmers began to trap and even shoot the monkeys. As a result several thousand macaques are culled annually in Japan – possibly one tenth of the total wild population; although as there has not been a population census since 1992, there is no accurate figure of how many wild monkeys exist in Japan today. This is probably the reason why the status of this species is listed as data deficient by the International Union for Conservation of Nature.

Several of the feeding stations created by researchers to lure monkeys out into the open have become parks where both scientists and tourists can observe the social life of snow monkeys. In addition to Jigokudani Monkey Park, there is Choshikei Monkey Park at the base of Mount Sentakubo on Shodoshima Island and Takasakiyama Monkey Park. However, as Japanese macaques begin to lose their fear of humans there is bound to be increasing friction between Japan's sole native monkey and the territory now occupied by humans. After part of Yakushima Island was elevated to a World Heritage Site, the increased publicity encouraged many more tourists to visit the island, thereby increasing the conflict between monkeys and mankind.

Above: Sign to Jigokudani Monkey Park at Shiga Heights.

Quite apart from Japanese macaques being extensively studied by scientists for six decades, these animals are firmly established in Japanese traditions and folklore. The Buddhist Tendai Sect based their three wise monkeys depicting see no evil, hear no evil and speak no evil on Japanese monkeys. For centuries they have been featured in paintings and in haiku (Japanese brief verses that often relate to nature).

Above: This wooden carving, which represents the three wise monkeys portraying 'See no evil, speak no evil, hear no evil', is based on snow monkeys. It can be seen at Nikko Toshogu – the mausoleum of Tokugawa Ieyasu (1543-1616) who founded the Tokugawa Shogunate, which ruled Japan for over 250 years from 1603 until 1868.
Photo by Imre Cikajlo/iStock

Haiku © Heather Angel 2009

swirling snow
hot pool macaques
ephemeral hats

Photo tips and hints

Ever since snow monkeys were featured in the 30 January 1970 issue of *Life* magazine, bathing in their own Jacuzzi at Shiga Heights near Nagano (now known as Jigokudani Monkey Park), tourists have made their way to this remote thermal valley. Few people venture forth on days when the sky darkens and snow clouds roll in, but this is precisely when striking pictures can be taken of emergent heads in the hot pool dusted with snow.

In the winter months, a lot of activity takes place around the pool area as monkeys come to drink, to warm up or maybe dive down for soy beans thrown in. As spring approaches, the monkeys spend less time in the pool, although they still come to drink. Early June is a great time to see the mothers with their newborn babies and the valley with a host of spring flowers.

On dull days a tripod is useful for steadying a long lens when using a slower shutter speed. If the action is fast and furious however, working with a hand-held camera or possibly a monopod, allows for a speedy way of changing the camera position. A zoom lens such as an 80-400mm or a 100-400mm allows for a rapid change of focal length for taking frame-filling shots of adults, family groups or mothers with their babies at varying distances. Before you depart, check out the view from the fixed webcam that looks out over the hot pool (see Information section). From here, a wide angle lens is useful for taking the whole pool with monkeys and the mountain slopes behind.

Above: The baby's body is a good average tone for spot-metering with a snow backdrop.

Left: An unattended tripod proves irresistible for a playful snow monkey youngster!

Opposite: Prefocusing on the baby's face helped to capture a fleeting facial expression.

Left: A youngster glances up into the lens as it tastes a new plant.

Opposite: A tight crop leads the eye to the two faces, framed below by the mother's arms.

It is quite possible to get pictures of the monkeys on a day visit to Jigokudani, if you spend the night nearby. However, a wider range of behaviour will be observed by spending several days there, getting to know the monkeys' habits so you can predict how they will react. For example, more monkeys are attracted to the viewing area at feeding times which are in the morning and afternoon. After feeding, they tend to disperse up the slopes. Just before the next feeding time they race down and any monkeys across the far side of the river have to cross back again using either the wooden planks or by leaping across the water.

During the early trips I was shooting transparencies, but since 2006 all images were shot as RAW using digital cameras.

93

Information and Acknowledgements

INFORMATION

Internet sites

More information about snow monkeys / Japanese macaques can be found on the following websites.

- **Primate Info Net (PIN)**

A Library and Information Service maintained by the Wisconsin Primate Research Center Library at the University of Wisconsin-Madison
http://pin.primate.wisc.edu

- **Jigokudani Monkey Park**

This park, located within a mountainous region of Nagano Prefecture on Honshu Island, is a popular tourist attraction. In winter, snow monkeys can be seen bathing and relaxing in the hot pool with infants playing on snowy slopes on a sunny day; in summer, the mothers have their newborn babies.
http://www.jigokudani-yaenkoen.co.jp/english/top/english.html

- There is even a live webcam overlooking the hot pool to view the monkeys' activities during daylight hours.
http://www.jigokudani-yaenkoen.co.jp/livecam/monkey/index.htm

ACKNOWLEDGEMENTS

Many people helped in the production of this book. Special thanks go to Bruno and Rika David who not only arranged my very first trip in April 1990 to see snow monkeys in the wild at Jigokudani, but also drove me there and came with me to Koshima Island – an unforgettable trip! Rika was my interpreter for talking to Mrs Mito during my visit to Koshima. Seiko Tsuchiya was a most attentive guide and interpreter for a winter 2003 Jigokudani trip when I was so ably assisted by the local tourist office arranging a jeep to the gate of the park and bringing along a sledge to transport all my gear to the Inn. Other trips were made to Jigokudani with Joe Van Os Photo Safaris, Keren Su of China Span and Zegrahm Expeditions. Lucy Simpson did a great job researching and also proof-reading the entire book, Ed Pugh was responsible for preparing all the digital images for reproduction and Kate Carter assisted with inputting copy and proof-reading. Alan Summers, a Japan Times Award winning published poet and a professional haiku writer, kindly read and advised me about my own haiku.
www.withwords.org.uk

FURTHER READING

• Fedigan Linda M. and Asquith Pamela J. (Editors), *The Monkeys of Arashiyama: thirty-five years of research in Japan and the West.* State University of New York Press, Albany, USA (1991).

• Iwago Mitsuaki and Iwago Hideko, *Snow Monkeys.* Chronicle Books, San Francisco, USA (1999).

• Rau, Margaret, *The Book of Pandas, Kangaroos and Snow Monkeys.* iUniverse.com Inc., Lincoln, USA (2001).

Other Wildlife Monographs titles published by

EM B Evans Mitchell Books

Wildlife Monographs
Giant Pandas
ISBN: 978-1-901268-13-3

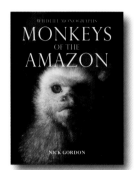

Wildlife Monographs
Monkeys of the Amazon
ISBN: 978-1-901268-10-2

Wildlife Monographs
Polar Bears
ISBN: 978-1-901268-15-7

Wildlife Monographs
Cheetahs
ISBN: 978-1-901268-09-6

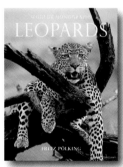

Wildlife Monographs
Loepards
ISBN: 978-1-901268-12-6

Wildlife Monographs
Sharks
ISBN: 978-1-901268-11-9

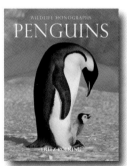

Wildlife Monographs
Penguins
ISBN: 978-1-901268-14-0

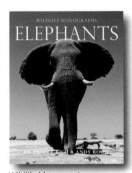

Wildlife Monographs
Elephants
ISBN: 978-1-901268-08-9

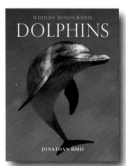

Wildlife Monographs
Dolphins
ISBN: 978-1-901268-17-1

Wildlife Monographs
Wolves
ISBN: 978-1-901268-18-8

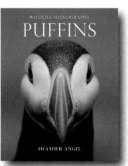

Wildlife Monographs
Puffins
ISBN: 978-1-901268-19-5

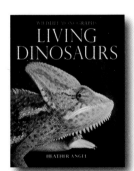

Wildlife Monographs
Living Dinosaurs
ISBN: 978-1-901268-36-2